# THE CAPTAIN OF THE BUTTERFLIES

# P.I.P.

*Cees Nooteboom*

# THE CAPTAIN OF
# THE BUTTERFLIES

*Translated from the Dutch by
Leonard Nathan and Herlinde Spahr
With an Introduction by Herlinde Spahr
and an Author's Note*

SUN &
MOON

CLASSICS

97

LOS ANGELES
SUN & MOON PRESS
1997

Sun & Moon Press
A Program of The Contemporary Arts Educational Project, Inc.
a nonprofit corporation
6026 Wilshire Boulevard, Los Angeles, California 90036
http:www.sunmoon.com

First Published by Sun & Moon Press in 1997
10 9 8 7 6 5 4 3 2 1

Some of the poems in this volume appeared originally
in *Vuurtijd, IJstijd* (Amsterdam: Arbeiderspers, 1984)
and *Het gezicht van het oog* (Amsterdam: Arbeiderspers, 1989)
Permission to reprint these poems was granted by the author.
English Translation ©1997 by Leonard Nathan and Herlinde Spahr
Biographical material ©1997 by Sun & Moon Press

This book was made possible, in part, through contributions to
The Contemporary Arts Educational Project, Inc., a nonprofit corporation.

The publication of this book was also made possible through a translation grant from
the Foundation for the Production and Translation of Dutch Literature.

Poems of this collection previously appeared in the magazines *Barnabe
Mountain Review* and *Crosscurrents: A Quarterly (Literary Olympians II 1987)*,
in Christiana Barrosa's *Koordinatennulpunk* (Galerie Schüppenhaur, Köln),
*The Berkeley Conference on Dutch Literature* (University Press of America 1987) and
*The Berkeley Conference on Dutch Literature* (University Press, 1993).
The author and translators wish to thank the editors of these magazines and books.

Cover: Simone Sassen, Photograph of public sculpture in Oviedo, Spain
Design: Katie Messborn
Typography: Guy Bennett

LIBRARY OF CONGRESS CATALOGING IN PUBLICATION DATA
Nooteboom, Cees [1933]
*The Captain of the Butterflies*
p. cm — (Sun & Moon Classics: 97)
ISBN: 1-557713-315-8
I. Title. II. Series. III. Translators
811'.54—dc20

Printed in the United States of America on acid-free paper.

# Contents

# Introduction

The work of the Dutch author Cees Nooteboom (born in The Hague in 1933) first came to the attention of the American public when his novel *Rituals* received the Pegasus Prize for Literature in 1983, a prize which provided for the translation and the publication of the work in English. Since then, six more novels have been made available in translation, novels which have established Cees Nooteboom in this country as a writer with a unique narrative voice, a voice that blends with ease the traditional strain of Dutch realism with the more cosmopolitan tradition of metafiction and postmodernism. The effect of realism in his novels is one created with mirrors, doubles, and looping plots, a world of shifting values and identities in which conflicting narrators vie for the readers' trust.

*The Captain of the Butterflies*, a representative collection of his poems, introduces Nooteboom for the first time as a poet to the English reader. Whereas his voice as a novelist could be silenced by crisis and personal turmoil (he did not write a novel for seventeen years before creating *Rituals*), the elliptical medium of poetry allowed him to speak, even when language itself seemed like betrayal. Starting in 1956, Nooteboom has published with regularity a large body of poems, altogether eleven volumes in Dutch. The poems not only span more than four decades, they also chronicle Nooteboom's evolution as a writer, documenting with almost painful urgency themes which he later introduces into his novels with a lighthearted flair.

The fissured, fragmented self, the dissolution of reality, the shrewd blurring of truth and semblance, these topoi of the postmodern idiom appear first in his poems as personal, existential insights that almost overwhelm the poetic voice itself. If the color red seems to be made up of paint in his novels, it carries traces of blood in his poems, memories of pain. That softly ironic tone which turns his narrators into such worldly, witty observers, is peeled away in his poems to reveal a poet who is completely alone, oblivious of the reader, focused on a world in which poetic meaning has taken refuge in the form of bleached, disintegrating skeletons, in the slower presence of a crumbling rock wall.

Nooteboom has often said that he considers himself first and foremost a poet. The reader who is already familiar with the more public voice of the novelist, with the wide range of his characters, the philosophical depth of his themes, will now be able to go behind the scenes to discover a writer who is more private and serious, a poet who is speaking with apparent honesty, albeit with the distortions, screens, and foils indigenous to the poetic medium.

The translation of these poems dates back to 1986 when Cees Nooteboom was invited as Regents' Lecturer to the Berkeley campus. I was a graduate student in the department of Comparative Literature, writing my dissertation, and though I was a novice at translating poetry, I was a native speaker of Dutch with a special passion for Nooteboom's work. Leonard Nathan was a professor in the Rhetoric Department, an experienced translator as well as a poet aware of the hazards of poetic language. Our collaborative effort was especially challenging since Nooteboom takes great liberties in Dutch, inventing new words, rupturing traditional syntax, favoring a style that is elliptical, even hermetic at times. The poet's own comments and elucidations often proved helpful in selecting the right alternative.

The poems collected in this volume represent perhaps a fourth of the number of poems published in Dutch. In our selection we tried to cover as many different periods and styles as possible, favoring those poems which survived best that shattering transfer from Dutch into English. The final grouping of the poems along thematic lines was determined by Cees Nooteboom.

—HERLINDE SPAHR

## Author's Note

The poems in this book have been selected from *Vuurtijd, IJstijd* (1984)—itself a selection of poems from 1955–1983—and from *Het gezicht van het oog* (1989), a title that is quite untranslatable, given its more than double meanings. *Gezicht* can mean "sight," "view," "vision," or "face," and the poems in this book concern different ways of seeing. *Oog* means "eye," so the title as a whole could suggest the "sight," "view," "vision," or "face" of the eye.

There are also more recent poems, some of them ("Mail," "Small Bang," "Tenth Floor," and "Meditation") written during my year as a Getty scholar in Santa Monica in 1996.

Accordingly, the poems in this volume represent different periods of my writing, many coming from early works of a period time in which I did not use capital letters and was very economic in the use of punctuation; though I would do it differently now, I did not feel I should meddle with my younger self, and I allowed the punctuation throughout the book to be inconsistent. If nothing else, it will enable the reader to identify those different periods.

I am immensely grateful to Leonard Nathan and Herlinde Spahr—both of whom I met during my stay as Regents' Lecturer at the University of California, Berkeley in 1989—for the time they have spent on this babylonic effort.

Leonard Nathan is a poet (*New and Selected Poems* [University of Pittsburgh Press] and *Returning Your Call* [Princeton University Press])—some of whose poems I translated into Dutch—and Professor Emeritus of Rhetoric at the University of California. Herlinde Spahr is an artist of Flemish origin, and lives in Orinda, California. She has a PhD. in Comparative Literature from Berkeley, and part of her doctoral thesis was devoted to my work.

—C N

*But now when I hear that there be three kinds of questions: Whether the thing be? What is it? And of what nature is it? I do indeed hold fast the images of the sounds of which those words be composed, and I know they passed through the air with a noise, and now are not.*

—ST. AUGUSTINE, *Confessions*
Book x, Chapter x
William Watts, 1631

# I

# SELF AND OTHERS

## Meditation

Trumpet blasts, that kind of morning.
The cat on her way to the office,
palm in prayer,
whisperings of dead souls
in the news from the capital.

Names, emptier than ever,
flapping against the window,
chittering loudly.
I look at the hands of the clock
like a nightwatch for days.
At my feet a lucid suspicion,
on my lap a double calendar.
I'm ready for anything!

Codes, sayings through a wall.
The man counting gets a grip on the semblance
of things: butterfly wings, lizard, cement,
the dirt, the repetition,

and more, and more,
a sum of untended time.

*Mail*

But then, are your ideas so clear
the mailman asked. Just at that moment
the sky darkened,
but that was another matter,
things around here happen that way,
from one moment to the next.

That means rain, he said, and it did.
Big drops. Behind him I could see the bay,
a plane leaden in the clouds,
slow. It landed.

Where do such seconds go?
How much rustling can be missed?
Which conversations cannot be
pulverized against the time-wall, in a lapse
of memory, somewhere at the bottom
of a dream?

Fiction, a house on a hill,
the psalm of rain, page six,
mailman, descent, downward path
into oblivion,
his, mine,
the fat of time

as someone might turn a page
without having read,

all written
for nothing.

## The Poem of Death

Along the cold thought of the moon
the light drifts
the wings of the birds are brilliantly painted

this is the poem of death
which begs and tumbles
in the long drawn arches of the evening,
nobody hears it.

nobody hears it, such winged sounds
fly right by the saints
silent, and stuck in the sand,
they are immobile in the drought.

on the hollow path
the painted birds.
in the carved white night
the enchanted voice.
among the swaying trumpets of the angels
those in masks whisper

a house is no house
a thing is no thing
life does not exist.

## Snow

As if it doesn't snow in your head!
As if for you too memory
is not like snow, snowing,
sifted down on all,
and all reshaped.

One thought of us
settles over the once so-sunlit view.
That doubling soft-sloped hill, out there,
in the curve, by the palm trees,
those two are us.

They lie there happy on the beach.
Books of ice, snowy cigarettes,
two remaindered tourists
in the lure of iceland,
burnt in crystal light.

So we forget ourselves,
tumble, white and silent,
over all past times,
we spin, floating, dancing,
over the white
of what is
not.

## In Memoriam Leo L.

Only a week ago
like a fetus in bed.
Real eyes, real nails.

Now, no longer curled up,
straightened by dead lumber
among sobbing daughters,

your smile a lock,
your black eyes behind their lids,
an indian far from his tribe.

Tomorrow the dance
of the odd priest,
Latin shaman
without magic,

only then the fire
of inaudible voices,
the eternal tracks

toward home.

## Riddle

The cricket is the monk of the bird.
His mother is the thistle,
his daughter a pebble.

And I? I build my nest
in the swaying seaweed
and swim into the riddle

where it is cool
and smells of time without end.

## The House on the Island

So many thoughts are sowed
in the garden around the vacant house.
I think of the empty kennel,
moonlight shining on it at night.

So let us dream. The cat has come back
with a moth in its jaws,
because it is summer.
So dream a different sky.

Soar over the house. It is shut.
Hunt the trees down. Thrash the blinds.
The ground is mum. I peer through cracks
at the mirror of an absent face.

The bed, stripped of its sheets,
is now itself asleep. The clock stands still,
time without will. The lawn chairs
lie on their sides. My empty house forgets me.

In my dream my house thinks only
of itself. It is a winter of cold
and of mildew. I come back in summer,
my feet older by ten months.

Bare feet on the red tiles
and the moon in the Bella Sombra.
Lizards under the lamp,
then why is my dream so somber?

In my life winters get longer, colors drain,
the fear in my friends grows stronger.
Love fades from my face.
I fold myself in a poem and wait.

## End of Season

It was a month like October.
The color of the wine faded,
the waiters drowned in the frozen
terrace.

This is the way the demon did it:
he sloshed through the marble water
and scooped her specter from the rock.

And this is how it seemed:
the wind came in from the sea
night in his wings.
The demon swept her shadow off
to a place I would never find.

And so he sealed the riddle that
she had been. He scorched my eyes and my ears
and broke the past.

Then, like prey torn
to pieces, he released her.
And me, me he let die
with the last tip of the year.

# Harbalorifa

So many forms of existence! So many creatures
to suffer and laugh in these stony hills!

The figtree is bent toward the south,
above us the soft snoring of a plane.

My friend is waiting near a bush with sharp thorns.
He knows the story of his fate,

we see the glitter of the sea
among gallnuts and thistles, a sail in the distance.

Everything sleeps. Give me some other life and I won't take it.
Shells and crickets, my cup is full of eternal noon.

The stream I drank from yesterday was cool and clear.
I saw the laurel tree's reflection, I saw the shadow

of the leaves drift away across the bottom.
This was all I ever wanted. Harbalorifa!

My age hangs on a thread. So I am the spider
above the path, weaving its polygonal time

from bramble to bramble,
until the wanderer passes on his way to the port,

the wanderer who strikes with his cane.

## Sleeping Gods

Taciturn as the mouth of shells,
between praying dogs and the irreverent
fluting of light,
the gleaming gods spoil in their gold-lacquered beds
wild and useless in their loneliness.

Outside, their antiquated horses stand waiting.
The jewels have been stolen from the chariots.
The saddles sit empty, empty the chariots,
coated and ruined by a mildew of space.

Only under the black night
the faithful crawl up to the walls of the house
and warm themselves at the immortality of their masters.

But the morning's white teeth
find everything, offerings and horses.
The square of the world is empty, empty the space,
a thousand years the gods sleep and then, another thousand,
dreaming the merciful salt of death.

## The Sealed Riders

Hole in the dark
they named the light of moon
and with their hands disfigured by it
they wanted its measure

and became a new movement
an army of rags with veiled faces
hidden in crowns and coats
on horses of human flesh.

They did not bear names
other than their own
some years they are invisible
eyes mouths ears all sealed

there'll be no end to this procession

I see them, see them
and burn.

## The Captain of the Butterflies

1

There is the captain of the butterflies!
All days hang under his bituminous wings.
The look of the air is vacant.
No one flies so noiselessly as this chieftain.

Haze over the great ovens.
The water consumed.

Suddenly the wind stirs
a sound between his insignias,
he alters direction.

Observed from the ground:
he is a black and plumed machine
with weapons and teeth.

2

Flesh and distance stalk each other in his thought.
The eye of his eye is canceled.

He is the absentee
who is there.

In the cabinet of the sky
his breathless uniforms wait.
His courtiers follow.

3

This is the eighteenth day.
Flourishing his wings in domes
of consuming stillness,
he surveys the destruction.

He imitates the movements
of a creation.
Thousands will follow.

He says:
If only once I could kill somebody,
create somebody.

Reality is the greatest contagion.

## This way

It could have been this way:
something filthy longs for something dirty
for the morning,

the painted rose
wants to be in the masterpiece.

The small begs for something smaller yet
for the road,

the big goes shopping
at giant shops.

It is so hard to defend yourself.
You see the butterfly, already bigger by a hand,

you see the flowers plowing soil,
the worm as snake.

This is the weight
that bursts the scales.

To have shared all that

with time as a hairdo,
as a god of a short-lived universe.

That, dear friend, was life
and it is what it was.

*Lock*


The water follows him.
The dead accompany him
though he knew no one.
He seals the wounds
and memory.
He seals the lock.

Is he inside or out?

There, briefly, something pale, a
horse composed of two people,
a seduction that seduces itself,
a sorrow that mates with itself,
and, hesitating between mirror and maze,
picks confusion
and cold.

Nothing clear. A hand which stretches,
a cigarette, someone, music, a cocoon of words.
A public and a secret man
in front of the hazy mirror,
in front of the sealed lock

he is inside and out.

## I Maschi

The masked rowers
came for him,
    in their boat
the bowl that must not break,
    the terribly fragile bowl
made of shining earth.

They knew the
darkness in which he moved,
    they were his
fate and his ill-fate.

He stood still, saw
on the stone beach the crows
    that always scared
the other birds away
    saw how the spider's web
became a weathervane's veil
    and heard the water.

It was all endless.
His shadow between the overturned boats,
    the driftwood against the pier.
The rowers shipped their oars,
    docked, and stepped onto land.

Then he heard the inaudible breaking
of something as fragile as eyes,

a sight he would never again see.

## No one

The invisible received more and more names,
the blind man always more power.
How he wandered and called out to his echo!

which called back with the call of a gull.
Now he still seeks the same statue
between banners and distances.

Sounds blow to the other side of the river.
No one stands there.

Nothing takes shape. The papers melt,
the photos fade. The stone is wax,
the script ash, time takes itself
and repeats the appearance

until his life becomes a mirror
in which he dissolves and evolves
but in which no one will be reflected
because there is nothing to see.

# The Fighters

1

He stuns himself at these encounters.
On white paths, no rain, he sees me,
their specters snap at him.

His freckled hands on the trellis,
he stares at him, stares,
wrapped loosely in the coats of my later disease.

He knows him, all those crowns and heads he puts on and off.
And behind my drifting eyes the dismantled streets
in which he thinks, of him.

2

It is a slow struggle of two men,
the same.
The fire hesitates. Ropy silence
sticks to their blows.

He always approaches him, bared,
to discard me.
He recognizes him, flinches,
then yields.

He tears my photo
and starts bleeding.

3

He kills himself
and exchanges names.

Killed and unraveled he sees his tracks.
I measure them: he still writes,
and in his scrawl.

4

We will meet again
and trace each other in the mirrors.
There is nothing pretty about these poems.

He stands there, laughing,
and waiting. He stands there, bleeding
and waits.

I stand there, waiting
and laughing. I bleed
and I wait.

*Self*

So established in its solitude
like a shipwreck cast in bronze.

Thus he looks at the healthy
on their eternal fields
at the end of the universe:

other people in an absent world
in which his gestures count for nothing,
his words are not true.

In his life the objects are called something else,
in it one buys a cure with homemade wealth
of straw and tears.

There circles refuse to be round,
and numbers don't fracture.

There the end is an end by its
self.

*Midday*


It takes so little.
Midday of glittering hours
that will not fit together,
and himself cut up by himself,
sitting in various chairs
with almost everywhere a soul or body.

In one part of the room is night.
Somewhere farther off simmers pasts, vacations and wars.
On the ceiling the sea touches the shining beach,
and no hand that controls all this,
no equerry, no computer,
only forever the same-self, self-same, he,
someone, somebody scattered,
the uncollected persona
in converse with himself, dreaming and thinking
present, invisible.

Someone who would go off to eat and sleep.
Someone with a watch and shoes.
Someone who had left.
Someone who was about to leave.

Someone who would stay on for a bit.

## Portrait, Self-portrait

Can he ever,
more enigmatic than a reader,
find the traces
of pardon or of poison
behind the window?

One of those two
rides the dark horses of my life,
one of the two
has me or will get me.

For many years
he hunts in the dark
and glittering landscape
like a light-giving sacrifice
in a shadow-hidden hunt.

And, as if I command the mist
from behind a clear panel,
I have made an intellect
from the dark
unveiling the veiled
until I became what I looked for,
irretrievable, invisible

like a man next to a statue.

## Churchill's Black Dog or Mr. Nuszbaum Complains

I who have no pupils,
and no servants.
I who eat my cheese alone
and see the wrong people
in the wrong cities.
I smell flowers in ice
and see death on a swing.

I who am quite aware
that a word is only a translation,
a poor code
among secretive services,
I myself have inherited at least
ten thousand words
from the large brothel
toward which the world empties.

I who have learned
that the Future is a motor
which has never yet run,
that all languages observe the same silence
and that all my private dreams
are on view in the movies

I,

and even that, not much longer.

## One Thousand Nights and Days

Like a king on a primitive island
the wind strides up and down the evening.
I hunt my invisible life,
the wings of my eyes burning.

Birds darken.
A brass twilight echoes in the mountains.
Peace grazes under the wooden trees,
but no one believes it.

Every bush conceals a soldier.
The grit of rain licks at the water.
Brass spreads its stain and sinks away.
I fly alone uneasy in my guilt.

Never will I meet my own body,
Kept from it by a shameful curtain.

## Abschied

Not for someone else,
this foolishness,
but for you.

When the high-rise is gone, when this is a plain,
and you a statue, self-raised,
and I touch you,

When all things suffer like me,
nailed down with sorrow, when to know nothing
is to sneak like a fungus through tissue

you stand still, silvered, splattered, the eastwind vagrant
around you, and around me,
I made a disaster out of the ordinary.

I'll forget everything about you, except you.
You rage through the space I occupy,
your love is fate.

Through your likeness I see the longing
from which we were expelled. I had offered everything,
you had refused everything. You had offered everything,
I did not see it.
Quiet now.

Death is a male disease.
You go around and gather up life.
Now quiet.

# II

# TRAVELS AND VISIONS

## Moment in Arcadia

The landscape is painted
in a blind eye.
The shepherds of noon,
their shell-like eyes sealed up and hardened,
sleep in stones of sun.
Monument in arcadia.

Their classical bones
support the order of life.
Only crickets argue for death,
urns of annihilation.

Birds of black gold fly up
and scatter their wings.
The always blinder painted eye
sees it and writes.

*Bogotá*

Three at night.
I drag this naked life along
as a fisherman his net along the bank,
heavy with water and dead fish
making trails with their own blood.

Three at night.
So I wake up in foreign towns,
hear how the rooster is beaten a third time
because in the dark he saw light.
Sorrow doesn't shun me.
I charm it with pompous words.

Three o'clock at night.
Stuffed and shut, square boxes of
silence surround my bed.
But that silence stings
a pain that cannot pass.
Silence levels the path on which
the messenger makes his rounds
saying that tomorrow it will be night again.

And then
I comb my bones, gather them up,
stride toward yet another passage, step into the water
and live.

*Fuji*

1

Here, on the slow, scalloped flanks,
the wooded, sorrel slope, snowwhite,
with the fine traces of priests and poets,
shining or somber in the floating world around it
it drifts or sails above swirling mists
like a form without weight,
like a peak of light.

2

Here, armored with walls of ice, seen
through the eye of a child among radiant blossoms,
in the black sack of the night, on the mirroring water,
from the dancing deck of a ship, against the windows of cars
        and trains,
it stands and guards among clouds and winds invisible, visible,
wanders along through the skies like a drifting bird
or settles on land like a state.

3

"Here," the traveler can say a thousand times to that fluid dream,
"here," the painter paints and drowns in his double landscape,
"here," the fisherman whispers patiently on his footbridge of
bamboo, "here,"
"here," and always they see something different

and with their high butterfly tones of uu and ee
their mouths form the name of the mountain that keeps his
      house there
and like a sun or a moon appears, disappears.


   4


There, etched in Yamanaka like a fire under water,
under the silk rains of Baiu, in the basket of summer,
weather-stained like a statue standing with its feet in the sea
it blows after storms and clouds on the flute of its craters.
There, with the highest eye in its tower,
it is the first to see goraiko, the purple blowhole of morning,

the departure of the traveling sun, the high spinning of stars.
All of Japan hangs on it like a gondola full of dreams
which it lifts and cherishes and carries along
through the sky
beyond the tract of time.

## *Fraulund*

Hair on an invisible skull,
buried in the field.

Night wanderer,
afraid of his reflection, afraid

of the invisible skull
as big as the world,

crushes an animal of moist asphalt
under the soles of his boots,

walks over the stain that he is
in ravels of moonlight,

high guardians the trees
combed by the night wind,

protect owls and hedgehogs
do not protect people,

people are animals out of dreams
that do not recognize themselves,

they turn in the darkness,
facing their own teeth.

## Rockface

I have been here for just an hour
and you call me ancient.

Your century is my instant.
Though you think me hard,
I feel myself flow.
You of flesh,
I of stone.

Both concealed in words,
we name the self-same thing.
Because your life is brief, mine is long
but there is no difference.

And yet,
once I was not here long before you were not here
and once, I will disappear, broken and crushed,
like you, unraveled, carried off
without a trace.

In my slow fossil thoughts
I know the same pride,
the same fall.

*Sun*

This is my most famous charade,
how in the evening I still hang in the air
and disappear in the distance as myself.

My color I leave behind
like a trail of blood on everything.
I've done this before.

That way I made the eyes
with which you can see me,
and the water in which you were born,
a little fish of a thing, armless and legless,
until the morning you crawled onto land
where nature was ready for you,
until the evening you stood erect
like a ruined beast with a lens.

## Rockplant

Wherever you see me,
in one or another form,
an animal in armor
a plant like a stone
I am the will.

In the most northern village on earth,
in the grave of a city, the frayed fire
of deserts:
where no one can live I exist
and I do that alone.

I make my food from grit,
water from marble, fire from ice
cured, burnt, and tortured
in the emptiest blazon of the world
I bear life,

and I am.

## Poseidon and Amphitrite, Villa Stabia, Pompeii

That infatuated moment
when heads are not yet skulls
the gods not yet dead

when they race over the sea on high-mettled horses
when their slaves under tiled sails
hunt for lobster

and I who find only fish
in the market
never again holiness

only the sea still ticks, sighs and sloshes
but allows the fragrance of the riddle
to fade

in a world turned bald and lonely
like the corpse of a gull on a rock

in a time that remains like a measure
now that eternity is dead

the overshadowed repetition
of a detail lacking majesty.

## Athena, Painted on an Amphora by Psiax (Brescia)

The unwise owl on your shield resembles a dove!
Among somber animals and ornaments
you extend your hand to the battle that no one
can see.
Along the straight pleats of your peplos
the lance slowly rises like a phallus—
it is you, the better half of Pallas!

Now morning turns evening, noon turns night.
Heracles kills the lion, Heracles is given a drink,
Heracles wears the mask.
And you, a face like a figurehead, protected him!

Everywhere connections, fabrics and filaments!
I hear you in the crickets on Hydra,
I see you in the mirror of the galini,
under the pale Peloponnesos, on the other shore of the sea
when all is peace—
and I feel again the shudder of years gone,
the shudder of your name, your helmet, my youth
and your eternal calm—

and my time ends like Satyricon:
a weathered fresco on a vacant, unkempt hill,
the instruments out of tune or smashed
and no one to measure how slowly the colors fade.

## Sphinx in the Museum at Delphi

My eyes are blank,
my face disfigured.
my eagle wings shed,
my lion body vanished.

Time made me, time ruined me.
the terror of my judgment has faded,
I live only
as a word on your tongue.

Now I am as blind
as the man who killed me,
now I pose no more riddles
than the one you can see:

the taut, broken, obdurate,
skull of a doll.

## Ibiza 60

Again we had ourselves locked up
on this god-forsaken island
planes no longer land here
now that it rains so hard
and the boats of the Compañia
arrive hours too late.

even in the garden of summer
armed winter prowls, knife in beak
wind leaps through cracks in the wall
and the path over the hill
is full of yellow mud and it rains, rains.

and we, we lie in bed
and read the first chapters
of the books we've already read, no
desire for more.
we listen to the bite and smack of the sea
and smoke up the whole deadstill
room.

memories of other summers and other winters,
of drinks and friends, of other, colder days
lazy I lie in bed and think

o will a ridiculous
and fragile old age finally
free us from these left-over
lies.

## Qui'amiyat Dikakah

I have seen you far below
When I was still a falcon, perched and praying
Above your coolness, your scales, your scurf,
Above your bed of stones and hunger
And your borders that are nothing
Cracked, sprung, split
In your desert skins, your rivers
of gravel, your herdless sands
You are forever stored away
In the chamber of my eyes,
And you will stay with me, waiting
Until I am the first to die.

## To Shiraz

How much time, how much thirst, how many days?
In drought I think of roses,
In a silence full of thistles I think of breasts,
Cupolas of glazed gold.

A traveler through a hundred deserts
is a traveler through one.
He repeats the verse of the poet
on the beads of this thought:

One more sentence, one more day, one more line
Till I can reach you again.

## A Ruin at Oulad-Merzoug

All the voices in me have vanished
and the births.
The dead have taken away their death.
The living have taken away their name.
I am broken stones,
crumbled memory.
I watch only over myself,
and I tell you:
time is the first to wear out.
What seemed long lapped itself up.
Wind and desert, the fury of things
all the forgetting,
it slowly eats me out
like a rat a cadaver.

## Altiplano

I am the messenger, spurred ahead
from portal to portal,
A nameless horseman
With the king's word in his heart.

In darkness the sound of dogs.
In daylight the sound of no one,
Agaves guard the distance with blades,
The palace of hatred.

The toad's soft feet
The snake's false script
These riddles I understand,
They are inscribed on my skin like a name:

One day you will never escape.

## Traveler

In the tormented reeds those two women
wrapped in their coats.
They've been there for centuries.
Tonight they govern my fears.

And you, devil of my poisoned dreams,
you who follow me and confound me
on an Oriental evening like this,
what do you want?

So many things I have not learned,
I only know myself inversely, the fugitive
running toward me,
pursued by retribution.

Two Japanese women, in a cyclone
seen by someone else, preserved and branded
in a firestorm of blisters.

What is this?

I am a traveler, looking only for rest.

## Sea

What you imagine is my voice, that rustling and complaint
that's how you gainsay me, you
who long for my silence.
I sway, luxuriating, a sacred landscape,
blessed even without your words, turned into myself.
Your hunting adds nothing to me,
you are nothing but your questions.

No, it is quite different,
even without you I have to be, but now that you're here,
those brief moments, I am the music.
You are only the strings.

Now try to dissolve me,
make your tones of water and mist,
sway with me in this light,
in my last, obscured rhymes,
and sit down and write.

## Trinidad

This I have often been:
a man on a road,
a man on a plane,
a man with a woman.

And this I have often been:
man who wanted to hide
under stone
to avoid seeing light.

These two men
carry my luggage,
read my papers,
eat my bread.

Together we travel the sound
and air of the world
in search of the invisible statue,
in which the three of us will meet
in the form
of one.

# III

## POEMS AND FICTIONS

## Small Bang

The poem heard how it was composed,
it saw the giant hand
from which it seemed to have its being, word by word,
it barely could keep up with itself.

Keep up, it saw itself spelled out, and its own echo,
keep up, keep up, but the hand
had run ahead, lashed by the whip
of its own scratchings,
that homesickness for form.

It hurts not to be whole
for someone who arrives out of nowhere.
The words lie breathless on the desk,
the hand disappears, returns, disappears,
the poem remembers nothing.

And the head, so far above,
still unrecognizable,
except as the mask of chaos and beginnings,
turns from its lines,

and listens to its own breathing,
the cadenza of thought
that ends the poem
with a sigh.

## Basho I

Old man in the middle of reeds suspicion of the poet.
He goes his way to the North he composes a book with his eyes.
He writes himself on the water he has lost his master.
Love only in the things cut out of clouds and winds.
This is his calling to visit friends as a farewell.
To gather skulls and lips under swaying skies.
Always the eye's kiss translated into the fit of words.
Seventeen the holy number in which the apparition is sealed.
Time consumed to a butterfly frozen in stone,
In a tide of marble the sheen of cut fossils.
Here the poet passed on his way to the North.
Here the poet passes forever once.

## Basho II

We know the cheap perils of poetic poetry
And of moonstruck singing. It is embalmed air,
Unless you make stones of it that glitter and give pain.
You, old master, cut the stones
With which you can kill a thrush.
You carved from the world an image that bears your name.
Seventeen stones like arrows a school of silenced singers.
See by the water a trace of the poet
On his way to the inmost snow country. See how the water
        erases it
How the man with the hat reinscribes it
Saving water and footstep, always arresting lost motion,
So that what vanished remains as something that vanished.

## Basho III

On his hat of cypress he wrote: *Nowhere in this universe*
*have I found a settled home.* Death took his hat off.
As he should. But the line stayed with us.
Only in his poems could he live.
*A little time and you will see the cherry blossoms of Yoshino.*
Set your sandals under the tree, lay your brushes to rest.
Tuck your staff in your hat, fashion the water in lines,
The light is yours, so too is the night.
A little while, cypress hat, and you too will see them,
The snow of Yoshino, the ice cap of Sado,
The island that embarks for Sorēn over gravestone waves.

## Basho IV

The poet is a mill that turns the landscape to words.
Yet he thinks like you and his eyes see the same.
*The sun that crashes in the mouth of the horse.*
The outer temple of Ise the beach of Narumi.
He sails in the canvas of mourning he sets course for his mission.
His jaws grind the blossoms down to the meter of poems.
The account of the cosmos as it presents itself daily.
In the North he knows himself a bundle of old clothes.
When he is where he never can be you still read his poems.
He peeled cucumbers and apples he painted his life
*I too am tempted by the wind that allows the clouds to drift.*

## Ybañez, Aquoy

"What does the light seek in the shade
but itself?"

This winter day
I saw the light skating,
a man dancing with his soul.

Here the fight with forms
armed from the arsenal,
the calamity of someone else's balance
tilted inward,
a hunger for sliding scales.

And then a final redemption?
No, harmony sleeps against the wall
in an always hidden thought,
its mission the eternal quest,
its conclusion the answer:

the question undone.

# Cartography

*for Cristina Barroso*

I

Only the bird sees what I see,
the impassable ways in my hand,
a golden and ash-colored beauty,
the surprising accident
of a world drawn only once,
a thought construed of matter,
a painting missing its painter,
my secret universe.

Oceans, steppes, volcanoes, the humming
of their names from always younger mouths.
My making hand follows their forms,
vein, chasm, slope, ravine,
the hidden lines of strata and ore,
diary of desert, of wilderness, of mirroring sea,
that which I am.

II

Ice age, star time,
my past exists in locked-up images,
called out by fire and water,
a registry of resin and sand.

That is how I show myself,
how I hide myself,
in ciphers of height and depth,
layers of color
on an atlas as big as the world.

III

Measure, says the book of maps.
Measure, given.
Measure, real
But given by whom?
Real for whom?

The tiny plane hovering above the shoreline,
shadow of Phoenician sails,
constellations, plumb line, calipers, ink,
the slow page from Strabo,
the prows of Aeneas, Odysseus,
or how the sea changes to paper,
the waves into words,
the exacting task of shrinking,
the art of meter and time.

IV

The inner spectacle
piles question upon question.
Were the dogs visible on that spit of land?

The death of the flies, poison of the flowers,
the track of the enemy,
the surveyor in his hotel?
Who followed the train with the future dead,
measured the slowness of the way?
Fate is not set down on maps.
Fate is all ours.

Grids, shading, scale, the constraint
of coordinates, words of magic
for the world as a thing.
But I go with my living earth
of rivers and marshes, bends and willows,
which I compose in my image.
When I retrace them I leave my seal,
a map painted
of soul.

## The Page on the Lily

The page lies on the lily,
and on the leaves of the lily.
The poem is all mirrors.

And he,
he sits there posturing on the edge of his grave
and listens to the gulping of time
in the poem across from him,
the never-to-be-grasped.

The page lies on the lily
and on the leaves of the lily.
The room is all mirrors.

I am in all mirrors.

## Golden Fiction

Look! The fires unfold.
The heathens fight again for a handful of ashes.
Tomorrow I leave again on my ship.

They are buried, my friends.
Under the trees their bodies persist.
Their souls rustle in many
leaves.

I hang my face in the wind
and astonish myself. Why am I so sad
if I expect nothing more than to stare at fires
and a ship's departure?

The traitor sits in his room and writes it down.
Out of which lives does he write? Which time?
Will the real life ever come to him
and take him with it?

No it will never take him with it.
The traitor sits in his room and writes
what the voices tell him.

## Homer on Ithaca

The day is serene, the buzzard sways over his prey.
A great box of silence
is being unpacked.

Over the shimmering bowl of the sea
the other island floats.
All the light is from porcelain
a fragile vase around us.

Yesterday it is happening again.
Today the hero is going to war.
Tomorrow he is coming back.

No, here nothing has ever changed.
Under the olive tree the blind man sleeps invisible
and hides in his eye the secret of the poet.

Sing, heavenly Muse!

## Nighthour

I write
the way my kind does
among the regalia of daily life
in a poem that seems translated
from the Spanish
so stiff and innocent.

Unimaginable how,
on such nights,
that which I call reality
puffs itself up:
the clock not ticking
but croaking like a frog.

Only the poet holds still
and peels the skin off the hours
clock, poet, frog,

and despises time.

## Bait

Poetry can never be about me,
Nor I about poetry.
I am alone, the poem is alone,
and the rest is for worms.
I stood on the streets where words live,
books, letters, reports,
and waited.
I have always waited.

The words, in light or dark forms,
transformed me into someone darker or lighter.
Poems passed me
and recognized themselves as a thing.
I could see them and see me.

Never will there be an end to this addiction.
Squadrons of poems in search of their poets.
They range without command through the vast precinct of words
and look for the bait of their perfect,
closed, sealed, composed,
and inviolable

form.

# *Writer*

1

At the far end of a dream
lies a harbor with palm trees
but all is disaster there and treason.
He was absent.

The iceman is twelve and sells poison
the ships are seaweed
the sea is a mirror of rotting glass.

The peasant women are afraid
they run out of their huts from the market
and each pulls a tombstone over her head.

2

Wrong! Transparent!
They do see the armored clouds,
the plane with flames and swords
the angels of ruin.

Peace! Peace!
Fatherland and death!
In the smoky air the poor steal
tomatoes and grapes from the deserted stalls.
He sees a moth on the wall

pretending to be a butterfly,
he hears the hobnails of the police
on the marble asphalt.

3

Nowhere more safe than the Hilton.
He fluffs his pillow and writes a little poem.
Death and life, love and a secret,
the pits of the fruit, it is all in there.
It is recited for the radio, the television
the commander comes and reads it

it is carved in the monument

he is gilded in public.

4

It is finished.
Immortal, he sits on the grass
next to the economist, the campesino, the guerillero
and smokes a havana
till his lips bleed.

Now he too,
together with many a scholar and slave,

is a victim of the revolution.

## Court, January

Images on the desk, the place where I read,
bookends, Chinese lions, roaring ebony,
bulging eyes, curved fangs, a moving fury,
scarcity of sonnets.
Still no poems observed this year.

Goethe, postcard, mining, Apollo, wrong age.
Eckermann knew: toothless.
A civil servant of considerable beauty.
Word thinker, satanic verses, silk lapels,
brow of plaster and posthumous life.

Zurbarán, courtier, painter. Monks,
habits, violence. The wrong side of the time-wall.
Cold fire, neglected ecstasies, treason
to the enduring flesh.

Only painted bread is still edible,
a thought as bitter as art.

## Scholasticism

This is the oldest conversation on earth.
The rhetoric of water
explodes against the dogma of stone.

But at the invisible closure
only the poet knows the outcome.
He dips his pen in stone
and writes on a table of foam.

## Cauda

Look at things, see them
in their metaphysical innocence,
not certain they exist.

Remember that discussion
in the bower, Nordic summer,
hydrangeas, the essential frog,
roses, masks.
Incense without a church.

A butterfly flies up in China
and changes a stormfront in Finland.
Someone said it. You were silent.
This you already knew.

When do paintings shed
the painter, when does the same matter become
a different thought? The evening fog stole across
the grass, drowned lawn, fountain,
windows.

Music, the splash of oars.
Someone turns on the light, someone
has no faith in dusk.
The question without answer
drifts around the house.

# IV

# THOUGHTS AND THESES

## Tenth Floor

Odysseus, never been here.
Here we are more cunning, more subtle
without the declension of myth.
Here no one's name glitters
forever and the seers turn
inward, traveling without maps.

Where have they gone?
Without their light, no company,
no shadow across the altar.
We eat the offerings ourselves,
meals without magic.

The sphinx knows our secrets,
as we do hers, no,
we pay the ferryman
long before we die,
before we vanish for good

and on time.

*Silesius dreams*

Dreams are true because they happen,
untrue because no one sees them
except for the lonely dreamer,
in his eyes that are only his own.

No one dreams us while we know it.
The dreamer's heart keeps beating,
his eyes compose the dream, he is not
in the world. He sleeps inside and outside
of time.

The soul has two eyes, so he dreams.
The one looks at the hours, the other
sees right through them,
to where duration never stops,
looking is consumed into seeing.

## Grail

Remember the time
that we were searching for something,
something quite precise,
a concept, paraphrase, definition,
a theme, thesis, supposition,
a summa of what we did not know,
something we wished
to assume or measure or tally
between all things obscure?

You know, don't you know
how we always wandered off, dividing
the concept and the quest,
Augustine the brothels, Albert the numbers,
Jorge the mirrors, Immanuel home, Pablo the forms,
Wolfgang the colors,
Teresa, Blaise, Friedrich, Leonardo, Augustus,
always tallying and measuring between words and notes,
        thinking
among nuns, soldiers and poets,
breaking, looking, splitting,
till the bones, the shadow,
a glimmer, a narrowing down
in senses or images,

until in a glass or a number
but always so briefly
a hiccup of a thought, of a way,
so endlessly vague became visible?

## The friends of Thales

They sat near the wine-black water
when the world was still silent,
men with speaking mouths
secure in their names that endure,
their raiment full of questions.

They saw the sun follow its rounds,
the moon in repeating changes
the world had to be known
for the book without script.

They counted the grit of the stars,
they combed the air with their thoughts.
Without answer the search withers,
without question the answer shrivels with thirst.

Not until later would they write
the how and why of the heavens:
through a sequence of endless veils
the pain of an end,
the slowest sense of a start.

## Xenophanes

You said it, I see it:
the imprint of a laurel leaf
on a rockface on Paros,
the petrified fish in the mountains
in his marbled water.
The proof inscribed in stone
swims nowhere now.

You said it, I hear it:
we are born out of earth and water,
out of water and earth is all that
is born and grows.

And I, with my better knowledge, would still
trade my inherited wisdom for your answer.

Asking is so much nobler than knowing
that I pity all that I know.

## Empedocles

The way nothing arrived back then
no one arrived there.
The way they only spoke then
to themselves.
A tower of stones with falcons,
flying stones near a granite coast.
The way fire burned there,
reflected in the surf.
The way nothing arrived back there,
no one arrived then.
The way words came like holy dogs,
at the call of their master.
The way souls came into the house of their life,
at the end of their rope.
The way that time began there
with fire that scorched the earth.
The way back then the house in the water.
The way a sky filled only with fire.

## *Latin*

In a dark wood, surely,
and well beyond the middle,
I had no further need
for a vernacular.

Nothing I had to say
could find an echo there,
my words had once again become
Latin, illegible, sealed.

Poet, clerk, secret deacon
of the smallest parish,
the averse sect of veiled meaning,
turned inward,

a gnosis of masked sayings
in a script ever more obscure.

## Plato, Meléndez

Plato was right,
Meléndez proves it.

Cheese, cherries, prunes,
jug,

because of beauty inedible,
unfit for use,

long before our thinking
exemplary,

without thinker
or painter

fated forever
to appear,

*the* cheese, *the* prunes,
*the* cherries, *the* jug.

## Lucretius

In the house of your body one poet,
One thinker. The poem is one cosmos,
The world one word.
Your thought was the chance stroke
In inevitable lines,
Your letters atoms.
Cicero had it right, though he did not know:
The twenty one letters of the alphabet
Still write your name.

*Fire*

The noon was lead,
Hare slept, partridge dreamt
Hunter's death, and
Spider wove the webs of Euclid.

And yet. Under the trees the seed
Of the fire brooded,
Sprang up, broke loose, ran round like
A rabid wolf, howling and
Snapping at nests and cobwebs.

What was left was ash, and the wind,
When it came, swept through the
Iron shimmer of the carbon trees,
Strewed its air in the
Silence, and

The fire's flower had shed
its flowers.

## Atoms

Take out of the shy square
Of your thoughts
The red of motion,
See how it falls in the empty stable
Of space with drops of
Luminous parts,
Always prevented from union
With other things,
In the unthinkable dream of the nothing that exists
Without substance.

So he thinks and writes, sealing
His thoughts with words, till they are there and
Exist in this book of the sleeping
Cosmos.

# The Earthly Course of Justice

We learned it in this way:
In the first course under our ivory
Roof the manifold Muses live
Divided in equal portions in
Confusing love.
Two books that do not read each other.

A cook knows his business: soak,
Drain the blood. But they are stubborn.
Each half governs itself,
Only in the pan are they alike.

This was not yet a problem for you,
Titus Lucretius Carus.
You served art as knowledge,
Knowledge as art, a skillet full of
Beauty and wisdom.

Cosmos, body, atom, infinite space
Weighed out and sautéed in hexameters, like
Einstein playing the violin, like
Da Vinci dissecting a womb.

## Twoness

Marriage of body and soul, how
The one always penetrates the other,
Sorrow has the face of pain,
Sickness masks itself with anguish, how the wish
Alters the thought, how they endure
Each other's form, and the death of one
Steals into the other, how in this pair
Of inextricable twins one always suffers with the other
Till the body finally breaks like a vase and
The soul spills out of it like water.

That way you broke the vase of your self
With the hand that wrote your book, and
Your soul flowed out
To where I can read it.

*Reflection, reflector*

So quick is the image that you send out
That it creates a second you:
A man of flesh sees
A man of bronze who stares back.

How fully you are scattered
Till out of invisible parts
You visibly are again
like the other you are
With whom you share this name.

It's nothing that you were ignorant
Of the speed of these reflections,
That they were a you you sent out and
Caught again in the pool of your eyes,
That you saw all this and proclaimed it
In the high tide of your hexameters,

That amazingly mattered.

## Finis Terrae

At last the earth stripped of all the voices of women,
her face turned away from the moon,
she chose the deeper mourning of emptiness,
left her ceaseless course and wandered
through the opened mouth of the cosmic seas,
a leaf on the great river.

Forgotten the names of animals and humans
she carried the graves of gods through
suddenly nameless halls.
No one who tallied or reaped, no one who shaped or wrote,
no one left.

All the paint peeled away, the letters
let go and burned, only the turning remained,
which once was time
and became time without number
flung from its home,
the time without time of death.

## *Tree*

Be me, become me
for once in your turbulent life.
From two continents
the wind arrives to cling,
dancing with me like a man.

I don't have
but I am my soul.
In the speech of my constant thought
I sigh, sway and whisper,
the exemplary tree
with its one-word tongue.

It is not only the monks
that sing like people,
I must always wait here
suffering for the wrong of the world
in my unrepeatable form
of innocence.

## Animal Skeleton

Whatever was inscribed in me is now revealed,
translated into different signs.
My bones declare the transfer
of life into death.

But I am still not gone.
Among the living flora
and the bite of rock
I edge toward dirt.
Then only can you call me nothing.

So read me once again
in this slow-motion mating.
Follow my sentences again
until I make no sense,
and, senseless, I await you.

## Last Act

A hundred times you wanted to think about the eye,
like our time by the sea,
looking at the sun,
as long as you could.

It closed with the same scene
of now and always, the bloodshot eye
that sags down from its strings,
behind the whisperings of the prompter.

But your inner eye saw it otherwise
and you dream up a sect that believed in this:
the world as eye that sees itself
with nowhere a circumference,
a basket full of holy apples
the eternal fruit of light.

The sect of creation as creator
existing through sight.

## Order

The gods are mortal,
but cannot die. Behind
their windows reigns untamable chaos,
master of nothing.

There water turns to fire, sea
floats through the air, there elements
lick the sight from one another's
eyes, there the law of chance breeds

a law without logic, the accident
that leads to vision,
the apple that falls in flames
like an airship, the counterfeit waltz of the hours,

the end without end.

*Harbalorifa,* p. 29: Medieval exclamation out of a poem by Duke Jan of Brabant.

*Churchill's Black Dog etc.,* p. 46: The Dutch for Nuszbaum is Nooteboom.

*Basho,* pp. 76–79: These poems have their origin in Basho's work and a trip I made with Dutch painter Sjoerd Bakker to Japan. The result was a permanent exhibition of Bakker's watercolors and etchings with my poems at the Department of Dutch Literature at the University of Amsterdam. The lines in italics refer to lines of Basho himself. Sado is an island, Sorēn is Russia, seventeen the number of syllables in a haiku. "Only in his poems could he live" alludes to a famous poem of Dutch poet J. Slauerhoff (1898–1936).

*Ybañez, Aquoy,* p. 80: refers to Spanish painter Miguel Ybañez, living in Aquoy, the Netherlands.

*Cartography,* pp. 81–83: poem written for a German exhibition of the work of Brazilian painter Cristina Barroso (Koordinatennullpunkt, Cologne and Munich 1996) who makes her paintings on maps.

*Court, January,* p. 91: "Satanic verses" in this case refers to Goethe's Faust.

*Plato, Meléndez,* p. 105: This Platonic poem was written "after" a famous still-life by Meléndez.

*Lucretius:* The Lucretius poems (pp. 106–111) all refer to passages in the work of Titus Lucretius Carus, who lived in the first century BC. According to St. Jerome, the poet committed suicide; though this is not certain, his suicide is the theme of "Twoness" on page 110.

Born in 1933 in The Hague, Cees Nooteboom is a poet and novelist, as well as a writer of works of travel. Living in Amsterdam, he has published numerous books, among them *Rituals, Philip and the Others, In the Dutch Mountains, The Knight Has Died, A Song of Truth and Semblance, Mokusei,* and *The Following Story. Rituals* was awarded the 1982 Pegasus Prize for Literature, and *The Following Story* was the winner of the 1993 European Literary Prize for Best Novel. Harcourt, Brace recently published his *Roads to Santiago: Detours and Riddles in the Lands and History of Spain.*

# SUN & MOON CLASSICS

PIERRE ALFERI [France]
*Natural Gaits* 95 (1-55713-231-3, $10.95)

CLAES ANDERSSON [Finland]
*What Became Words* 121 (1-55713-231-3, $11.95)

DAVID ANTIN [USA]
*Selected Poems: 1963–1973* 10 (1-55713-058-2, $13.95)

ECE AYHAN [Turkey]
*A Blind Cat Black* AND *Orthodoxies* 125 (1-55713-102-3, $10.95)

DJUNA BARNES [USA]
*At the Roots of the Stars: The Short Plays* 53 (1-55713-160-0, $12.95)
*The Book of Repulsive Women* 59 (1-55713-173-2, $6.95)
*Collected Stories* 110 (1-55713-226-7, $24.95 [cloth])
*Interviews* 86 (0-940650-37-1, $12.95)
*New York* 5 (0-940650-99-1, $12.95)
*Smoke and Other Early Stories* 2 (1-55713-014-0, $9.95)

CHARLES BERNSTEIN [USA]
*Content's Dream: Essays 1975–1984* 49 (0-940650-56-8, $14.95)
*Dark City* 48 (1-55713-162-7, $11.95)
*Rough Trades* 14 (1-55713-080-9, $10.95)

JENS BJØRNEBOE [Norway]
*The Bird Lovers* 43 (1-55713-146-5, $9.95)

ANDRÉ DU BOUCHET [France]
*Where Heat Looms* 87 (1-55713-238-0, $12.95)

ANDRÉ BRETON [France]
*Arcanum 17* 51 (1-55713-170-8, $12.95)
*Earthlight* 26 (1-55713-095-7, $12.95)

DAVID BROMIGE [b. England/Canada]
*The Harbormaster of Hong Kong* 32 (1-55713-027-2, $10.95)

MARY BUTTS [England]
*Scenes from the Life of Cleopatra* 72 (1-55713-140-6, $13.95)

PAUL CELAN [b. Bukovina/France]
*Breathturn* 74 (1-55713-218-6, $12.95)

WENDY WALKER [USA]
  *The Sea-Rabbit or, The Artist of Life* 57 (1-55713-001-9, $12.95)
  *The Secret Service* 20 (1-55713-084-1, $13.95)
  *Stories Out of Omarie* 58 (1-55713-172-4, $12.95)

BARRETT WATTEN [USA]
  *Frame (1971–1991)* 117 (1-55713-239-9, $13.95)

MAC WELLMAN [USA]
  *The Land Beyond the Forest: Dracula* AND *Swoop* 112
    (1-55713-228-3, $12.95)
  *Two Plays: A Murder of Crows* AND *The Hyacinth Macaw* 62
    (1-55713-197-X, $11.95)

JOHN WIENERS [USA]
  *707 Scott Street* 106 (1-55713-252-6, $12.95)

ÉMILE ZOLA [France]
  *The Belly of Paris* 70 (1-55713-066-3, $14.95)

*

Individuals order from:
Sun & Moon Press
6026 Wilshire Boulevard
Los Angeles, California 90036
213-857-1115

Libraries and Bookstores in the United States and Canada
should order from:
Consortium Book Sales & Distribution
1045 Westgate Drive, Suite 90
Saint Paul, Minnesota 55114-1065
800-283-3572
FAX 612-221-0124

Libraries and Bookstores in the United Kingdom and on the Continent
should order from:
Password Books Ltd.
23 New Mount Street
Manchester M4 4DE, ENGLAND
0161 953 4009
INTERNATIONAL +44 61 953-4009
0161 953 4090